PATHFINDERS
IN EXPLORATION

Exploring Deserts

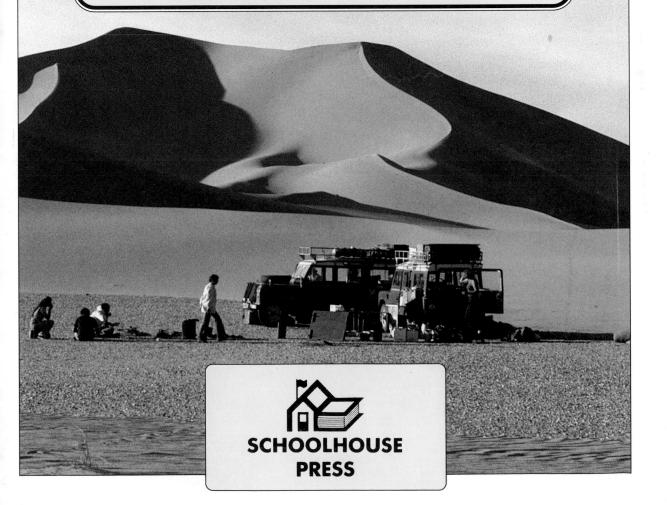

SCHOOLHOUSE PRESS

Copyright © 1988 by Schoolhouse Press, Inc.
160 Gould Street, Needham
Massachusettes 02194
ISBN 0-8086-1160-7 (hardback)
ISBN 0-8086-1167-4 (paperback)

Original copyright, © Macmillan Education Limited 1987
All rights reserved. No reproduction, copy or transmission of
this publication may be made without written permission.

No paragraph of this publication may be reporduced, copied
or transmitted without written permission of the publishers.

Authors: Derek Cullen and John Murray-Robertson

Editorial planning by AMR

Designed and typeset by The Pen and Ink Book Company
Ltd, London

Illustrated by Eugene Fleurey

Picture research by Faith Perkins

Printed in Hong Kong

88/89/90/91/92/93   654321

Photographic Credits

t=top b=bottom l=left r=right

The author and publishers wish to acknowledge, with thanks, the following photographic sources: 28*t* J Allan Cash, London; 39 Barnaby's Picture Library, London; 15, 26-27, 36*l* BBC Hulton Picture Library, London; 38 Bettmann Archive, New York; 10, 13, 17*b*, 18*l* and *r* (courtesy of Lady Anne Lytton and the British Library), 36*r*, 40*t* BPCC/Aldus Archive, London; 11*t*, 28-29 Bridgeman Art Library, London; 25*l* (Stein Collection) The British Library, London; 42 Church of Jesus Christ of Latter Day Saints; 23 (photograph Marcus Brooke), 34 (photograph Penny Tweedie) Colorific, London; 22*t* Courtesy of Curtis Brown; contents 11*b*, 33*t* Mary Evans Picture Library, London; 25*r* (reproduced from Buddist Cave Paintings by Basil Gray) Courtesy of Faber and Faber; 12 (portrait of Alexandrine Tinné by H A d'Ainecey) Haags Gemeentenemuseum, The Hague; 8, 14 Sonia Halliday Photographs; 8-9, 17*t*, 41, 43 Robert Harding Photographs, London; 6 Michael Holford; 26-27 John Massey Stewart; 5*r*, 7, 29, 31, 32, 33*b*, 35*t* and *b*, 40*b* Peter Newark's Western Americana; title 5*l*, 37 Picturepoint (UK); 16-17, 20*b*, 21, 22*b* Royal Geographical Society, London; 20*t* John Topham Picture Library

Cover photograph courtesy of Picturepoint (UK).

The publishers have made every effort to trace the copyright holders, but if they have inadvertently overlooked any, they will be pleased to make the necessary arrangement at the first opportunity.

Note to the reader
In this book there are some words in the text which are printed in **bold** type. This shows that the word is listed in the glossary on page 46. The glossary gives a brief explanation of words which may be new to you.

Contents

Introduction

In this book, we are going to look at some of the people who risked their lives in the dry lands we call **deserts**. Deserts are the areas of the world where there is little or no rainfall year after year. There are places in some deserts where it has not rained for years. Deserts are **barren**. Very few plants or trees can survive there because water is so scarce. Not many animals can live where there is so little to eat or drink.

There are different types of deserts. There are rocky deserts like the Great Basin Desert in the United States. Some deserts are sandy like the Arabian Desert. This desert stretches from the Red Sea to the Arabian Gulf.

▼ These are the main desert regions of the world. Deserts cover about one seventh of the land surface of the earth. Only about five percent of the earth's population lives in deserts.

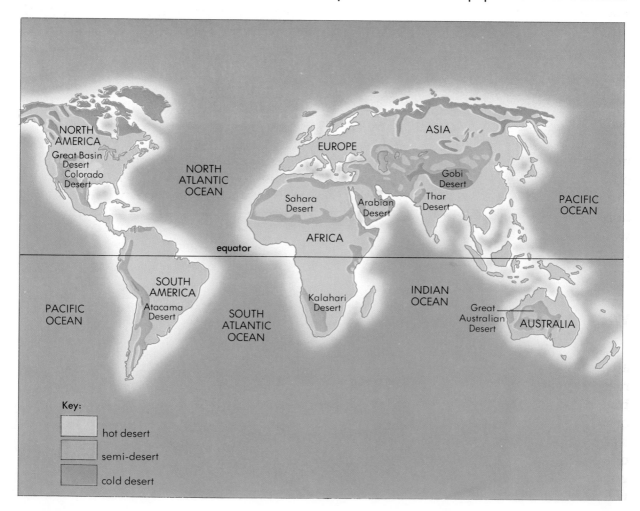

NORTH AMERICA
Great Basin Desert
Colorado Desert
NORTH ATLANTIC OCEAN
EUROPE
ASIA
Gobi Desert
Sahara Desert
Arabian Desert
Thar Desert
PACIFIC OCEAN
AFRICA
equator
SOUTH AMERICA
Atacama Desert
SOUTH ATLANTIC OCEAN
Kalahari Desert
INDIAN OCEAN
Great Australian Desert
AUSTRALIA
PACIFIC OCEAN

Key:
hot desert
semi-desert
cold desert

▲ These desert people are traveling through the Sahara Desert in Algeria. Camels have been used for hundreds of years to carry people and food from one oasis to another.

Desert People

Most of the people who live in the deserts of the world do not spend very much time in one place. They are called **nomads**. These people move around in order to find food for themselves and their animals. They travel from one water hole to another. The fertile area around a water hole is called an **oasis**. Sometimes, there is enough water at an oasis for people to live there all the time.

Why Explore Deserts?

Over the years, people have been attracted by the deserts for many reasons. Some early explorers were **traders**. They hoped to set up safe ways, or **routes**, across the deserts. These routes took them to the lands where they bought gold, spices, salt, and other goods. Many of the early explorers wanted to draw maps to show the oases, the mountains, and other landmarks in the deserts. Sometimes, they just hoped to gain honor and fame for themselves and for their countries. There were other explorers who went out to make their fortunes. They looked for **treasure**, like diamonds and precious metals, in the deserts.

Not all explorers were looking for profit or fame. Some were attracted by the danger and the mystery of the desert. One explorer, named Wilfred Thesiger, explored the Arabian Desert about forty years ago. He was often tired and thirsty, but he said he loved the freedom and the way of life in the desert. He is like many explorers in this book. These people looked for lonely places to test themselves. They wanted to go into the unknown, even if they risked death by doing so.

▼ Francisco Coronado was an early Spanish explorer. In 1540, he set out to find gold and other riches, but instead found Native American villages in the southwestern part of the United States. Coronado explored the Rio Grande and central Kansas.

The Sahara Desert

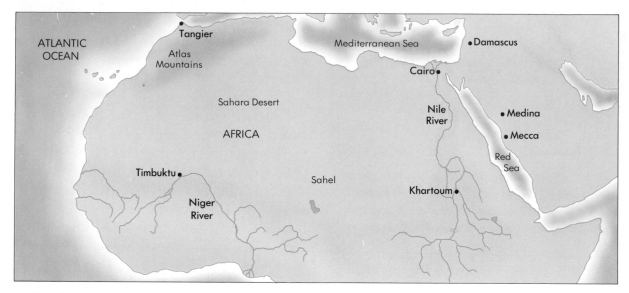

The largest desert in the world is the Sahara in North Africa. A lot of the Sahara is rocky sandstone land with high mountain tops, or **peaks**. Some of the peaks are covered with snow. In other parts, there are thousands of square miles of white sand. The Sahara is very hot. The average daytime **temperature** is 100°F.

Until recently, only nomads and traders traveled in the Sahara. The traders took goods from country to country. They traveled in groups for safety, from oasis to oasis. They took camels with them to carry their goods. Some groups of traders still travel like this today. A group of traders is called a **caravan**.

Other people cross the desert more quickly and easily in trucks. These trucks are built to travel on rough ground.

▲ The Sahara Desert stretches across northern Africa from the Atlantic Ocean in the west to the Red Sea in the east. From the north, it starts at the Atlas Mountains and goes to the Sahel region in the south. It covers parts of ten different countries.

Ibn Battuta

It was not an easy journey when Ibn Battuta set out on his travels in 1325. This rich Arab from Tangier in Morocco was a good **Muslim**. He wanted to follow his religion's rule. This rule says that Muslims should visit the holy cities of **Islam**, which are called Mecca and Medina. His first journey took him straight across the Sahara, and on to Damascus in Syria. There, he got married. Then, he went on to Mecca alone. He wrote about these journeys in his travel book, *The Rihlah*.

The Great Traveler

Battuta is known as "the great traveler of Islam." He went to many cities and even reached China. He also spent some time in East Africa. For two years, he lived on the Maldive Islands in the Indian Ocean. He covered 75,000 miles on his many journeys. People say he met sixty different rulers on his travels. He tried "never to travel the same road a second time." The extent of his travels was amazing for that time.

The Journey to Timbuktu

Battuta's last and most famous journey was, like his first, across the Sahara. He went from Tangier to West Africa and back. He wanted to follow the trade route. He wrote, "There is no road...

◀ This picture of Muslim pilgrims was painted over 750 years ago. They are traveling together on camels and horses on a religious journey. They may be going to the holy cities of Mecca and Medina.

▲ Ibn Battuta traveled all over North Africa. He also went to China on one of his journeys.

nothing but sand blown by the wind." Once, he was ten days from the nearest water. Somehow, he managed to reach a village. The people in the village were slaves who worked for the salt traders. All their houses were built of salt.

At last, Battuta reached Timbuktu, a city in the south of the Sahara Desert. From there, he went down part of the Niger River in a canoe. After more journeys in the area around Timbuktu, he went back across the Sahara to Tangier.

Battuta died in Tangier after thirty years of desert travel. He had used no maps on his journeys. He found his way by using the sun and stars, and by talking to nomads who knew the desert.

7

The First Explorers

The North Africans knew about the routes through the desert before maps were drawn. People have lived in the Sahara for many thousands of years. Some live in small towns built near the oases. They grow dates and **millet**, a type of grain, and they keep goats. The other people of the Sahara are nomads. They belong to the Beduoin and Tuareg people. Their camel caravans cross the desert carrying their tents, food, and clothing. The nomads trade in gold, dates, and meat **preserved** with salt. They also trade in **saltpeter**, which is used to make gunpowder.

▲ An oasis in Saudi Arabia where water is plentiful. A town has been built and crops are being grown. Oases have been centers of trade for hundreds of years.

▲ These camels are carrying salt, which is an important trade item to desert nomads. The traders and their camels cross the desert in a long caravan.

The Europeans did not find ways of crossing the Sahara until about 200 years ago. However, they traded for gold with the Africans on the west coast. They heard tales of splendid kingdoms inland, which were supposed to be filled with gold and precious jewels. The Europeans wanted to find these kingdoms and treasures.

The Europeans also traded in gold, silver, and slaves on the east coast of Africa. They wanted to find an overland route from west to east. By finding an overland route, they could avoid the sea route around the Horn of Africa. Pirates attacked ships often in these waters.

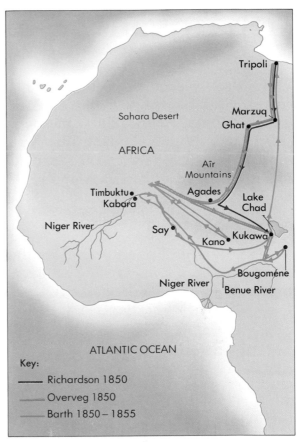

▲ The routes followed by James Richardson, Heinrich Barth, and Adolf Overveg.

The Unknown Continent

Early maps show how little the Europeans knew about Africa. Traders from Europe knew of a way inland from the west coast to Timbuktu and Lake Chad. However, about 150 years ago, people in Europe wanted to draw better maps. They also wanted to study Africa in order to get to know more about the rivers, the mountains, and the peoples of Africa. Some people set up **expeditions**. They sent out groups of people to find out more about this land, or **continent**.

Expedition to the Niger River

One of these expeditions was set up in Britain and led by James Richardson. His aim was to find out about the area, or **region**, around the upper part of the Niger River. This region is on the southwest edge of the Sahara Desert. Richardson wanted to map the cities and caravan routes in the area.

At this time, people could not go all the way up the Niger River to Lake Chad and Timbuktu. This was because they did not know where the mouth of the Niger was. So Richardson decided to cross the Sahara from the north. In 1850, he set off for Timbuktu with boxes of goods, or **supplies**, loaded onto camels. He even took a boat which was in two halves. He was going to use it to sail on Lake Chad!

9

Richardson's Expedition

Richardson picked the people for his journey very carefully. He chose two Germans to go with him. One was named Adolf Overveg and the other was Heinrich Barth. Barth had studied geography, and could speak Arabic well.

South to Lake Chad

In 1850, the group left Tripoli on the Mediterranean for Lake Chad. They traveled to Marzuq and Ghat, two oasis towns in the heart of the Sahara Desert. From there, they went across the Air Mountains to Agades. They were in constant danger from the Tuareg people, who often stopped them to ask for money. Barth also found it hard to get along with Richardson. They had many arguments.

When the group reached Agades, they split up. Richardson went southeast to Kukawa. Barth and Overveg went west to map the area east of Timbuktu.

Barth often set out to explore places on his own. Once, he went by himself to find the city of Kano, now a part of Nigeria. He dressed in Arab clothing and dyed his face. He did this so he could get around more easily among the local people. Barth liked the city of Kano. There were about 30,000 people living there at that time. He found out a lot about the people, and came to respect their way of life.

Barth rejoined Overveg, and they went off to Kukawa to find Richardson. When they reached Kukawa, they found that Richardson had died of a fever. The two Germans then set out to explore the area south of Lake Chad. They traveled as far as the Benue River, which flows into the Niger River. Both men spent fifteen months in this area. While they were there, Barth set off once again on his own. He went to the city of Bougoméne, south of Lake Chad. There, the local ruler put him in prison for a short time. When he was released, Barth rejoined his friend. Unfortunately, Overveg also died of a fever a few weeks later.

◀ A water hole in the Sahara Desert. The lives of desert explorers depended on oases and water holes. If a water hole went dry, the explorers could die of thirst.

Barth Alone

Barth was now alone. In November, 1852, he set off on a long journey west to Timbuktu. It took him ten months to get there. As he traveled, he made notes of the things he saw and the people he met. At last, he reached Timbuktu. He found it a rich and busy trading city. The houses were made of brick rather than mud. This showed that Timbuktu was a wealthy place.

Barth spent another two and a half years in West Africa. Then, in May, 1855, he decided to return home. He left Lake Chad and went back across the Sahara Desert to Tripoli. After his return to Germany, he gave advice to many other expeditions. His maps were the best ones that people in Europe had ever seen of West Africa.

▲ This picture of Kano has been drawn from one of the sketches Heinrich Barth did on his expedition to West Africa.

▲ This is a painting of Heinrich Barth reaching Timbuktu. Timbuktu is in the southwest Sahara. Timbuktu used to be an important center on the trans-Saharan caravan route.

Alexandrine Tinné

After Barth's return to Europe, a Dutch woman set out for North Africa. Her name was Alexandrine Tinné. Like Barth and Richardson, she wanted to find out all about the Sahara and its people.

Alexandrine Tinné came from a wealthy family in the Netherlands. She could speak many languages, including Arabic. This was very useful on her journeys in North Africa. She could also ride horses well.

The First Journey

In 1863, Tinné set out for Cairo in Egypt with a group of people. Her mother, her aunt, and six scientists were in the group. First, they sailed up the Nile River to Khartoum. They hoped to explore the area around one of the smaller rivers which flows into the Nile. This river is called the Bahr al-Ghazal.

▲ This is a portrait of Alexandrine Tinné. She was very adventurous and in her twenties when she went to Africa.

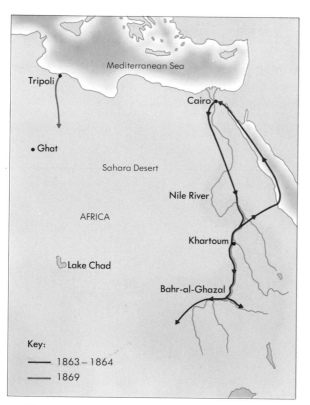

▲ The routes Alexandrine Tinné and her companions took on their travels in the Sahara Desert.

The journey was both hard and unhappy for Tinné. Both her mother and one of the scientists died of a fever. Another one of the scientists was killed by a water buffalo. After these sad events, the rest of the group decided it would be best for them to return to Khartoum. They had been back in Khartoum only a few days when Tinné's aunt also died of a fever.

Tinné did not want to give up. She was a brave woman. She decided to return to Cairo. There, she set up a **base**, from which she went on journeys to the western Sahara.

The Final Journey

In 1869, Tinné went to Tripoli in Libya. There, she joined a caravan which was crossing the Sahara to Lake Chad. The area they were to cross was controlled by the Tuareg people. Tinné hired two Dutch sailors to act as her bodyguards.

The Tuareg people thought that Europeans were their enemies. They often forced them to give up their goods and their money. This made it hard for any group of people to cross the Sahara in safety.

When the caravan was less than a quarter of the way to Lake Chad, they met a Tuareg **chieftain**. He and his men seemed friendly and helpful. They offered to guide Tinné all the way to Ghat. This was an oasis town in the heart of the desert. In fact, all the Tuaregs really wanted was Tinné's money.

▲ The Tuaregs are the largest group of people living in the Sahara. They often wear blue clothes which leave a blue color on their skin. They always wear turbans wrapped around their heads and across their faces, so that only their eyes show. This protects their faces from the burning sun and blowing desert sand.

Tinné had brought two iron tanks that were filled with water. Each day, the tanks were loaded onto the camels carefully. The Tuaregs were sure the tanks were full of gold coins. Some days after the Tuaregs joined the caravan, they attacked Tinne's group. The Tuaregs opened the tanks and found only water. They killed the two Dutch bodyguards, and the other people in the caravan ran away. Tinné was left alone and died in the desert. She was only thirty years old.

A Traveler in Lebanon

On the eastern Mediterranean coast are the countries of Turkey, Syria and Lebanon. A large part of these countries is covered by the Syrian Desert. A group of people called the Druze live there. These people kept themselves apart from others and did not welcome strangers. Yet, it was to this area that a British woman, Lady Hester Stanhope, went in the early 1800's.

Lady Hester Stanhope

Lady Hester was born in Britain in 1776. She spent most of her early life with her uncle who was a Prime Minister. She took care of him until his death. Hester had always wanted to travel. At the age of thirty-four, she set out for Turkey with her maid and a doctor. She brought a doctor because sickness was a European's greatest danger in the eastern Mediterranean. Hester's travels started in the city of Constantinople, which was the name of the capital of Turkey at that time. Now, it is called Istanbul.

◀ Lady Hester Stanhope's journeys in the eastern Mediterranean.

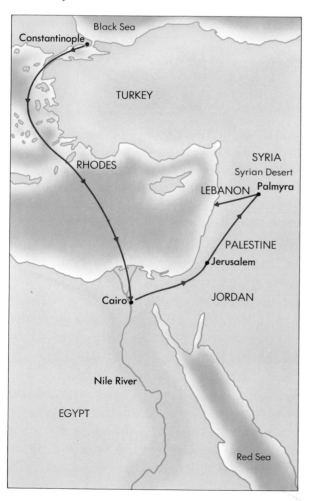

▼ This is Constantinople in Turkey in the 1800's. Lady Hester lived here for two years before she traveled to Egypt. Constantinople is now called Istanbul.

◀ Lady Hester Stanhope wore middle-eastern dress and followed local customs. She was popular with the local people and learned their languages. Lady Hester never returned to England. She preferred to stay in Lebanon.

From Rhodes, Hester traveled to Cairo in Egypt. From there, she went to Jerusalem in what was then **Palestine**. Her real aim, however, was to go to the Syrian Desert.

Travels in the Desert

By now, Hester had learned Arabic and other local languages. She wanted to visit the Druze. She was warned that they did not like strangers. Also, they had never seen a European woman before. However, the Druze liked and admired Hester. They thought she was brave to travel in the desert. They treated her with great respect.

Hester was very pleased when she was able to visit the ruined city of Palmyra. She had heard that three British travelers had been attacked while traveling in the area near the city. So she went dressed up, or **disguised**, as a Bedouin. She went in the company of a Bedouin prince. It was an honor to be taken to Palmyra, even though she had to go in disguise for her own safety.

Hester spent the rest of her life in the Lebanon. She shared all she had with the local people. She gave shelter to poor people in her house on Mount Lebanon. At the age of sixty-three, she died happy and loved by the people there.

Shipwrecked

From Constantinople, Hester, her maid, and doctor set sail for Egypt. Their ship was caught in a storm. They were lucky to land safely on the island of Rhodes. Hester's clothing was lost with the ship, so she had to wear Turkish dress. She found this loose clothing was better in hot weather than her tight European clothing. She wore that style of clothing for the rest of her life.

A Traveler to Mecca

The Arabian Desert lies east of the Sahara Desert across the Red Sea. Within this area, there are the Muslims' two holy cities of Mecca and Medina.

Each year, thousands of Muslims make a holy journey, or **pilgrimage**, to Mecca. No one but a Muslim can enter the holy city. The only non-Muslims who have been able to get there have gone in disguise. John Lewis Burckhardt was one of these non-Muslims.

John Lewis Burckhardt

Burckhardt was born in Lausanne in Switzerland. He wanted to explore the area around the Niger River and Timbuktu in West Africa. This part of Africa is Muslim, and in those days the people there did not welcome non-Muslims.

In 1809, Burckhardt went to Syria to learn Arabic. He also wanted to learn all he could about the Muslim religion. Then, he planned to go to Cairo in Egypt. There he would disguise himself as an Arab. In Cairo, he could join a caravan of **pilgrims** returning from Mecca to West Africa.

In 1812, Burckhardt reached Cairo. He could not find any pilgrims going west, so he set off to visit Dongola in the Sudan. Burckhardt was the first European to reach this area by crossing the Nubian Desert.

On his way back to Cairo, Burckhardt saw the famous temple of Abu Simbel. This is an ancient Egyptian rock temple with four carvings, sixty-five feet high, cut out of the rock.

▶ This is an early sketch of Cairo looking west over the Mohammed Ali mosque. It was drawn in 1848. Today, Cairo is the capital of Egypt.

▲ The ancient temple of Abu Simbel was carved out of the mountainside beside the Nile River in southern Egypt. It was built over 3,000 years ago by the Pharoah Rameses II. The carved figures which guard the entrance are of the Pharoah himself.

A Change of Plan

There was still no caravan going to West Africa when Burckhardt returned to Cairo. Therefore, he changed his plans and decided to go to Mecca instead. He joined a caravan and went to Shendi, which was a desert market town near Khartoum. There, he joined a group of traders, or **merchants**. They were going to a port on the Red Sea called Suakin. From Suakin, Burckhardt crossed with pilgrims in an open boat to Jeddah, in Arabia. In Jeddah, he met an Egyptian named Mehemet Ali. Mehemet knew about Burckhardt's travels and admired him. He told the local people that Burckhardt was a Muslim. This was not truc, but his story made it possible for Burckhardt to enter the holy city of Mecca.

In 1815, Burckhardt got back to Cairo after two and a half years of traveling. He never managed to go to West Africa as he had first planned. Burckhardt died in Cairo two years later.

▲ Mehemet Ali was a famous soldier who was Master of Egypt in 1805. Here, he entertains some Europeans in his palace in Alexandria.

The Blunts

▲ Lady Anne Blunt dressed as an Arab when she traveled. This made it easier for her to travel among the desert people. These clothes were also more comfortable in the desert heat.

Over one hundred years ago, Wilfred Blunt was working in Damascus, in Syria. He was a **diplomat** who worked for the British government. Blunt's wife, Lady Anne, was with him in Syria. They both loved to travel in the Middle East and North Africa.

The Blunts wanted to reach the city of Ha'il in the center of Arabia. Very few people from Europe had seen this city. It would be a long journey across the Syrian Desert and then across the Nefud Desert in Arabia.

The Blunts hoped they would see Arab horses on their journey. They had a **stud farm** in Britain where they bred racehorses. They wanted to buy some Arab horses and take them back to Britain.

A Bedouin Caravan

In 1878, the Blunts set off with a caravan of Bedouin traders. Many of the Bedouin did not want the Blunts to come with them. The Blunts were in constant danger of being attacked. However, a Bedouin chief, or **sheik**, was friendly to them. He had a lot of power and he was able to protect them.

The Blunts liked to write down an account of all that they saw and heard. Lady Blunt was an artist, and she painted pictures of the desert and the people she met there. Some of the desert people, called the Wahabi, did not like the Blunts making notes. They thought the Blunts might be spies.

▼ This is one of Lady Anne's paintings of a pilgrim camp in Arabia.

Once, the Blunts rode their horses far away from the caravan. They got off their horses to take a rest. Then, a group of Wahabi, armed with spears, came toward them. In a panic, Lady Anne tried to get back to her horse. She twisted her knee and fell. When Wilfred went to help her, the Wahabi seized him. They were about to kill Wilfred when their friend, the sheik, rode up and saved them both.

Buying Arab Horses

At last, the Blunts reached Ha'il. There, they met the ruler of the area. He was named Mohammed Ibn Rashid, and he owned many fine Arab racehorses. The horses were smaller than British racehorses, but fast and strong. The Blunts bought some of these horses and sent them back to Britain. Later, the horses were to father many famous racehorses.

The Blunts set out from Ha'il to Bushehr, a port on the northeast coast of the Persian Gulf. On their way across the Nefud Desert, they bought more horses to take back to Britain. Finally, they reached Bushehr. They had traveled 2,125 miles through hot and dry desert country since leaving Syria.

The routes of explorers in the Syrian and Arabian Deserts.

Key:
———— Burckhardt 1812–1815
– – – – The Blunts 1878
———— Thomas 1930–1931
– – – – Philby 1931–1932
———— Wilfred Thesiger 1930–1933

The Empty Quarter

By 1930, most of the world's deserts had been crossed and mapped. In Saudi Arabia, there was one desert which no European had crossed. This is known as "the Empty Quarter." It is a good name for an area of 155,000 square miles of **sand dunes**. Sometimes, these hills of sand are over 330 feet high. The Empty Quarter is burning hot during the day. At night, it is freezing cold. There are very few water holes. Therefore, people do not stay in the Empty Quarter for very long.

Bertram Thomas

Bertram Thomas was a British diplomat. He had been working and exploring in Muscat and Oman on the Persian Gulf since 1924. He wanted to be the first European to cross the Empty Quarter. Thomas planned to start his journey from the south coast. It was hard to persuade the Bedouin to guide him across the desert. At last, a sheik named Salih bin Yakut, agreed to go with Thomas across the Empty Quarter.

▲ The sand dunes in the Empty Quarter can be very high. The wind moves the sand dunes, so that the landscape can look different each day.

▼ Bertram Thomas, seated on the camel, with his guides in Oman in 1930. He was the first European to cross the Empty Quarter.

On December 10, 1930, Thomas set off with Sheik Yakut and their camels. He planned to reach Doha on the Persian Gulf. On the journey, they saw many sand dunes, and Thomas admired their shape and size. They also had to face **sandstorms**.

During these sandstorms, the wind blew the sand into their eyes, noses, and mouths. It was hard to travel when the wind was very strong.

As Thomas and Sheik Yakut got close to Doha, the Bedouin sang songs to their camels about water. The thirsty camels pricked up their ears and began to walk more quickly. They reached Doha on February 5, 1931. Thomas had crossed the Empty Quarter.

The City Destroyed by God

Another man from Britain, named Harry Philby, also wanted to cross the Empty Quarter. He wanted to find the ancient city of Wabar. The desert people thought God had "destroyed" the city because the people there were wicked. Arab travelers said that only a large lump of metal now stood where the city had been.

▼ Harry Philby photographed with the Bedouin tribesmen who traveled with him.

On January 7, 1932, Philby set off from Hofuf in the north with some Bedouin. He went south into the center of the desert. There, he found that Wabar was really two large holes, or **craters**, in the ground. They were about 330 feet wide and 33 feet deep. They had been made by **meteorites**. Meteorites are pieces of rock which travel in space. Sometimes, they hit the earth.

In one of the craters, Philby found a large piece of iron. It was the remains of the meteorite. Perhaps, this was the large lump of metal which the desert people believed was once the wicked city of Wabar.

Philby moved south across the Empty Quarter. Then, he turned west and finally reached the Suleivel Oasis. It was March 11, 1932. He had crossed the Empty Quarter. After Philby's journey, no European crossed the Empty Quarter again for fourteen years.

The Man Who Loved the Desert

People explored deserts for many reasons. Wilfred Thesiger went into the deserts because he admired the people who lived there. He liked the way they lived. Later in his life, he made two journeys in the Empty Quarter between 1946 and 1948. He wrote about his journeys in a book called *Arabian Sands*. He praised the courage and kindness of the people in that area.

▲ Wilfred Thesiger during his crossing of the Empty Quarter.

Wilfred Thesiger

Thesiger was born in Ethiopia in Africa. He made his first journey into the desert in 1930. He spent a month in the Danakil. This is a harsh desert area in northern Ethiopia. It is one of the hottest places in the world. Thesiger traveled on foot, and at night he slept under the stars. He was alone with no one to help him if he became sick. Often, he was tired, thirsty, and afraid. In spite of this, he was happy. He had found the magic and mystery of the desert.

Thesiger met the people who lived in the desert. They were armed with ancient guns, or **muskets**. They carried their guns across the back of their necks and hung their arms up and over the guns. This helped them to sweat less in the fierce heat and to breathe more easily. You can still see people carrying guns like this in Ethiopia today.

▲ This is the salt lake in the Danakil Desert. Wilfred Thesiger found the area around the lake very barren and very hot.

A Mystery Solved

Three years after his first trip, Thesiger went back to the Danakil. He managed to persuade the local ruler, or **sultan**, to let him explore an area no European had been allowed to travel through before. This area was around the Awash River. This river was a mystery. It did not appear to flow into the sea as other rivers do.

◄ Wilfred Thesiger sitting in the center with four Bedouin people. They are all armed with muskets.

Thesiger followed the course of the Awash and found that it ended in a large salt lake. On the surface of this lake, he saw red plant matter floating. Thesiger said this **algae** looked like dried blood. The whole lake looked gloomy. The only wildlife he saw were small **wading birds** and a few very small, yellow-eyed crocodiles.

Thesiger was lucky to survive his trips through the barren Danakil. The people there were well-known for their violent way of life. Even well-armed caravans of traders had been killed. This was the first of the desert areas Thesiger was to explore. He continued his desert travels all through his life.

The Gobi Desert

The Gobi Desert in Asia is one of the largest desert areas in the world. It stretches across most of Mongolia and borders northern China. It is surrounded by mountains to the north, the south, and the west. In the summer, it is very hot during the day, but at night, the temperature falls steeply. In the winter, it is very cold and there are snowstorms, or **blizzards**. There is very little water in the Gobi Desert. It rains very little and there are just a few streams and no big rivers at all. Most of the area is bare rock. In the summer, a little coarse grass and some thorny bushes grow. In some places, there is just enough grass to feed a few sheep, horses, and camels.

A Chinese Traveler

About 1,300 years ago, a young Chinese priest, or **monk**, set out from China to travel to India. His name was Hsuan-Tsang and he was only nineteen years old. He wanted to find out more about his religion of **Buddhism** from the Buddhist monks in India. The ruler of China had told Hsuan-Tsang not to go to India. The ruler was angry when he heard that the young monk had left with some friends and a guide.

The Gobi Desert lay ahead of Hsuan-Tsang. His friends and the guide all turned back. They did not want to risk crossing the desert, so Hsuan-Tsang went on alone. He had no maps or guide to show him which way to go. Luckily, he rode on a horse which had crossed the Gobi Desert many times before.

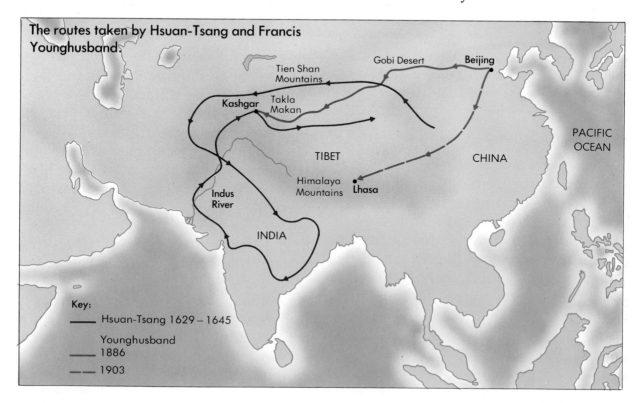

The routes taken by Hsuan-Tsang and Francis Younghusband.

Key:
—— Hsuan-Tsang 1629 – 1645

Younghusband
—— 1886
— — 1903

▲ This is a cave painting of Hsuan-Tsang. It was painted by Buddhist monks.

Across the Gobi Desert

Hsuan-Tsang tried to follow the tracks of camels and other animals. He was in danger of getting lost. Several times he almost died of thirst. Once, his **water bag** dropped and burst. He went for five days without water before he was saved by a sudden rain shower. Once, he was saved by his horse. It refused to go the way Hsuan-Tsang wanted and took him instead to a pool of water. Hsuan-Tsang said the pool was "as sweet and bright as a mirror." Later, he wrote about the Gobi Desert. He said, "There are no birds overhead, and no beasts below. There is neither water nor herbs to be found."

Sixteen years later, Hsuan-Tsang went back to China across the desert. He had spent many years in Tibet, India, and **Ceylon**, where he lived with Buddhist monks and traveled around. The ruler of China forgave Hsuan-Tsang and asked him to write some books about his journeys.

▲ This picture was painted over 1,000 years ago. It shows Hsuan-Tsang returning from his travels in India.

The Forbidden City

About a hundred years ago, the British Empire ruled most of India. The British were afraid that the Russians would try to move into Afganistan and Tibet which are to the north of India. Both the British and the Russians had tried to get to the city of Lhasa, the capital of Tibet. This was the home of the ruler, the Dalai Lama. It was hard for **foreigners** from other lands to reach the Dalai Lama's city. The local people attacked strangers. Also, the city was in a **remote** place. The Himalaya Mountains lay to the south. The Gobi Desert lay to the northeast.

▲ The Gobi Desert is treeless and rocky. It is the coldest, most northern desert in the world.

Francis Younghusband

Francis Younghusband was an officer in the British Army. In 1886, he was sent to Beijing in China. There, the British army allowed him to cross overland from Beijing to Kashgar. Kashgar was near the Pamir Mountains. It was a journey of about 2,000 miles to get there and he would have to cross the Gobi Desert.

On April 4, 1886, Younghusband set out from Beijing with only a guide, a Chinese cook and eight camels. In two weeks, they reached a small town on the

◄ The Dalai Lama was the supreme ruler of Tibet. He was worshipped as a god and thought to be holy. This is the thirteenth Dalai Lama, photographed when he was twenty-four.

▲ Francis Younghusband and his soldiers marching past one of the Tibetan fortresses.

edge of the Gobi Desert. There, they hired five more camels and a guide who knew the way across the desert. In order to avoid the hottest part of the day, Younghusband and his group began to travel each day at three in the afternoon. They rode their camels until midnight, and often used the stars to guide them. The air was very dry and created some strange effects. The group's blankets crackled and sparked with electricity when they spread them out!

Younghusband and his men said that they saw only a few brown bushes and no grass. They found water only in rough water holes which people in other caravans had dug earlier. The journey across the Gobi Desert took seventy days. At the end, the group rode for twenty-eight hours to cover the last seventy miles to an oasis.

After Younghusband left the Gobi Desert, he had another 875 miles to travel before he reached Kashgar. He had to cross another desert called the Takla Makan which is south of the Tien Shan Mountains. From there, he crossed to Kashgar.

Journey to Tibet

Younghusband was one of the few people to have crossed Central Asia from Beijing to Kashgar. It was because of this journey that the British decided to send him into Tibet to find the city of Lhasa. In 1903, Younghusband set out with **porters**, pack animals, and 3,000 soldiers. Among the animals were two zebrules, which are a cross between a zebra and a mule. The journey was difficult and dangerous. Many of the animals died, and there were constant attacks by the local people. At last, Younghusband and his men arrived in Lhasa.

The Australian Desert

While the Sahara Desert was being explored and mapped, people began to explore the vast empty areas of Australia. People had settled along the coastal regions. Most of them lived in the southeast of Australia where there was more rain. There, they built the towns of Sydney, Adelaide, and Melbourne. The inland region of the continent was largely unexplored up to 150 years ago.

Charles Sturt

Charles Sturt was one of the early explorers of the inland areas of Australia. He had watched birds flying north, so he thought there must be water inland. In 1844, he set out to explore central Australia. He wanted to find places where people could live. Sturt went with fifteen men, eleven horses, two hundred sheep and thirty bullocks. The group went up the Murray and Darling Rivers as far as they could then, north across the Main Barrier Range. In this area, there were only a few water holes.

It was summer, and the temperature rose to almost 120 °F. Matches caught fire, and the wool on the sheep stopped growing! The men and animals were saved when Sturt found a large water hole near Malparinka on January 27, 1845. There, they dug shelters under the ground and waited for the cooler weather. Then, Sturt tried to move

▲ Alice Springs is in the Northern Territory, and is right in the middle of Australia. This is the type of desert country around the town of Alice Springs that many of the early Australian explorers traveled through.

farther inland again. He found nothing but a rocky **wasteland**. Today, this area is called the Sturt Desert. There were no water holes, so the men had to turn back.

John Stuart

More people started to settle in Australia. The South Australian government wanted to put up a **telegraph line** across the continent. A reward of £2,000 was offered to anyone who could cross the continent from the south to the north.

John Stuart, who had traveled with Sturt, wanted to collect the reward. He set out from Adelaide with two other men. They crossed the Macdonnell Range in the center of Australia and reached what is today called Mount Stuart. There, they were forced to turn back because of sickness and a lack of water. The men had gotten within 300 miles of the **Gulf** of Carpentaria in northeast Australia.

▲ John Stuart was born in Scotland and had traveled with Charles Sturt into the interior of Australia. In 1861, he reached Darling after traveling from Adelaide on the south coast.

When Stuart got back to Adelaide, the government gave him money for another expedition. In January, 1861, Stuart set out again with thirteen men and forty-nine horses. This expedition was able to get just a little farther than Stuart had on his previous journey.

On a later journey, Stuart did reach the north coast. In July, 1862, he saw the Indian Ocean at the mouth of the Mary River on Van Diemen Gulf. He was very pleased, but his health had suffered because of the difficult journey. He died four years later.

▲ The departure of the British explorer, Captain Charles Sturt, on his expedition into the interior of Australia in 1844. Earlier, he had explored the Darling River and the Lower Murray River.

The Race from South to North

Key:
— Sturt 1844 – 1846
- - Stuart 1858 – 1862
— Burke and Wills 1860 – 1861
Giles
— 1873
- - 1876

Van Diemen Gulf

Gulf of Carpentaria

Great Sandy Desert

INDIAN OCEAN

Gibson Desert

Mount Stuart
Macdonnell Range
Alice Springs

Mount Destruction

Ayers Rock

Great Victoria Desert   Ayers Range

Simpson Desert

Cooper's Creek

Sturt Desert

Lake Eyre   Main
Mount   Barrier
Hopeless   Range

Malparinka

Darling River

Menindee

Perth

Adelaide

Sydney

Murray River

Melbourne

▲ The routes taken by the early Australian explorers. The four major deserts in Australia are the Simpson, the Gibson, the Great Sandy, and the Great Victoria. They cover about one third of the land area.

The attempt to cross Australia from the south to the north became a race. The state of Victoria set up an expedition. They chose Robert Burke to lead it. The problem was that Burke knew nothing about traveling in the desert.

On August 20, 1860, Burke and his group set off from Melbourne toward the north. Burke went with eighteen men, some camels, horses, and twenty-two tons of dried food and supplies. They pushed on toward Menindee, which was 400 miles north of Melbourne. They covered twenty miles a day. Burke gave an order that food should be left behind to help them travel faster. He even left behind the lime juice. This was a mistake. The lime juice kept the men healthy. It contained **vitamin C**. Vitamin C was needed to protect the men from a disease called **scurvy**.

Soon, it became clear that Burke could not gain the trust of many of his men. Before they reached Menindee, nine men had left Burke. Among them were the doctor and second-in-command, George Landells, who had argued with Burke.

▲ The beginning of the Robert Burke and William Wills expedition in Melbourne in 1860. The explorers succeeded in crossing the continent, but died of starvation on the return journey.

Toward Cooper's Creek

At Menindee, Burke chose a local man, William Wright, to wait for the rest of the supplies. These supplies were being sent up behind them. Wright was to join Burke with these supplies 400 miles farther north. Burke went on through the dry and rocky Sturt Desert to Cooper's **Creek**. He took seven men, some camels and horses with him. There, they set up a camp and waited for Wright to join them. There was water to drink and a little shade under the trees to protect them from the fierce sun. There were, however, hundreds of rats, so they had to hang their food in the trees. The men waited for five weeks, but Wright did not appear.

To the Gulf of Carpentaria

Burke could not wait any longer. He left a man, named William Brahé, and three others behind to wait for Wright. They were to guard the food they had left in the trees at the camp. Burke chose three men, William Wills, John King, and Charles Gray, to go with him on the last stretch of the journey. They had three months' supply of food with them, and some camels. After traveling north for 700 miles they entered a damp, soft, **swampy** area which the camels could not get through. Burke left the camels with Gray and King, and he set off on foot with Wills to travel the last thirty miles to the coast. At last, in February, 1861, they got to the sea. They were the first men to cross Australia from the south to the north. They had made a journey of over 1,500 miles.

A Hard Journey Back

Burke and Wills had crossed the continent. They were worried as they turned back to Cooper's Creek. It had taken them two months to get to the sea from Cooper's Creek. They had a long journey ahead of them, and they only had one month's supply of food left.

Burke and Wills met Gray and King with their pony Billy as they made their way back across the swamp. Burke told the men they would have to cut their daily **rations** of food in half. For ten days, they were slowed down by heavy rain storms. It took over a month for the men to cross the swamp into the desert. They were becoming weaker and weaker from lack of food. Gray could not walk any longer, and he finally died of weakness and hunger. After four months, Burke, Wills, and King made it back to Cooper's Creek.

At Cooper's Creek

Brahé and the three other men had waited for Burke at Cooper's Creek. Brahé had had a hard time at the camp. The rats had continued to eat the food, and the men were also weak from fever. Also, there was no sign of Wright, who was supposed to be coming with supplies of food. Burke had said he would be back in three months. After nearly four months of waiting, Brahé decided to go south to find Wright. He left a supply of food and a note for Burke in case Burke returned.

▲ Cooper's Creek was made into a permanent camp for Burke and his men. More food and more men were supposed to be sent to Cooper's Creek, but they arrived too late.

About seven hours after Brahé left, Burke got back to Cooper's Creek. He found the note and the food that Brahé had left. Now, he had to decide what was the best thing to do. He could try to catch up with Brahé, or he could try to get across the desert to a cattle station at Mount Hopeless. Burke decided to go to the cattle station, which was 200 miles away. He hid a small supply of food, and then left a note for Brahé to say where he had gone.

▲ Robert Burke, William Wills, and John King tried to reach Mount Hopeless to find help. They ran out of water and food and had to turn back to Cooper's Crek.

Brahé Meets Wright

Brahe went south and met Wright. They went back together to Cooper's Creek to find Burke. When they got there, they found no sign of Burke and his men. Brahé and Wright did not notice that the food Brahé had left had been taken. Also, they did not see the note Burke had left behind about his plan to find help at Mount Hopeless. They were sure that Burke and his men were lost forever.

▲ John King was to be the only survivor of the expedition.

Back to Cooper's Creek

Burke, Wills, and King could not travel as far as Mount Hopeless. They could find no water on the way, and they had no food left. Burke decided to turn back to Cooper's Creek. There, they could find water and the food which they had hidden. By this time, the men were very weak from hunger and from thirst. Sometimes, they were able to shoot a crow. At other times, they lived on the seeds of desert plants. Once, they met some local people called **Aborigines**. The Aborigines have lived in the desert for thousands of years. They have learned how to find enough food to eat and enough water to drink. Burke was afraid of them, and he fired his pistol into the air to keep them away. At lst, the three men struggled back to Cooper's Creek.

Help from the Aborigines

Burke knew he had to find help. There was not much food left at Cooper's Creek, so he set off again with King. They left Wills behind because he was so weak. Now that Wills was alone, the Aborigines came to help him. They shared their food with him. After a short time, Wills regained some of his strength. He set out again, and caught up with Burke and King. The small amount of food they had taken with them was gone. They were living on desert plants and seeds.

▲ These water-holding frogs provide water for the Aborigines. The frogs can survive a dry period in the desert of up to a year. They store water in their bodies and then bury themselves in mud. The frogs come up to the surface again when the rain comes.

At last, Burke decided to ask the Aborigines for help. By this time, however, the Aborigines had left their camp to go **walkabout**. Wills was now so weak that he could not stand up, so Burke and King left him again at the camp. They set off to try to find the Aborigines.

A Tragic Ending

Burke and King failed to find the Aborigines. Burke was now so weak he could not continue. He died on the 30th of June. As King stood by his dead friend, he felt he was being watched. There were several Aborigines behind him weeping. They took King back to their camp to find Wills. When they got there, they found Wills had died also.

The Aborigines fed and took care of King at their camp. About eleven weeks later, a rescue party arrived. The rescue party was led by Alfred Howitt of Melbourne. It was one of the four groups which had been sent out to look for Burke and his men. King was alive, but by this time he was so thin that he could hardly move. The Aborigines had tried to feed him, but he was already too weak when they found him. The rescue party took him back to safety, but he died two years later from poor health.

▲ John King sitting by the body of Robert Burke. It had been a successful expedition because they had reached the Gulf of Carpentaria in the north. The expedition, however, had a tragic ending.

▲ Eventually, the bodies of Robert Burke and William Wills were found. They were taken back to Melbourne and given a large funeral.

Across Australia

The continent had been crossed from the south to the north. Now, the race was on to find a route from central Australia to the west coast.

Ernest Giles

Ernest Giles first tried to cross from central Australia to the west coast in 1872. His first attempt failed. In 1873, he set out from Adelaide again. With Alf Gibson and two others, he started his journey west from Lake Eyre. This place is about 125 miles southeast of the town of Alice Springs. At first, the men traveled through a grassy valley which was full of flowers and birds. Then, they went on to Ayers Range, south of the Macdonnell Range. These hills were "huge, red, rounded blocks of stone." The only problem for the men was an attack by Aborigines whom they were able to drive off. The Aborigines may have attacked Giles because he and his men were getting too close to Ayers Rock. This is a holy place for the Aborigines.

Finding a Route

The country had grown drier and drier as Giles and his men got closer to Ayers Rock. They made a camp past Ayers Rock in a place where there was water.

From the camp, Giles went on alone to find a good route. He rode for about ninety miles but he was forced to turn back by the heat and lack of water. He did not realize when he turned back that he was only ten miles from water.

▲ Ernest Giles was born in Britain in 1835. He became a famous Australian explorer, and set out on four expeditions to the west coast between 1872 and 1876.

▲ Ernest Giles had to drink from any water holes he could find during his trips. Sometimes, the water was pure, often it was stagnant. The stagnant water would have made him sick.

It was almost the end of December when Giles returned to the camp. On Christmas Day, the men were attacked by Aborigines. Giles fired his rifle and they ran away. Giles led his men northward. On the route, they found a pool deep enough to bathe in. After that, they found no more water and their horses died. On reaching what Giles named the Mountain of Destruction, the men turned back toward Ayers Rock.

▲ Ayers Rock in the Northern Territory is one and half miles long and 1,140 feet high. It contains many small caves with rock paintings. These were made long ago by Aborigine artists.

The Last Attempts

Giles set off again to find a route from Adelaide to the west coast. He went with Alf Gibson, four horses, some food and forty gallons of water. After traveling sixty miles, they set two horses free to make their own way back. They also hung ten gallons of water in a tree for the return journey. The water was stored in small barrels, or **kegs**. They rode on for another 110 miles. This was as far as they could risk traveling without finding water. On the way back, one of the horses collapsed. Giles sent Gibson on ahead with the one remaining horse. Giles traveled on foot. He reached the kegs of water, and then he made the journey back alone to the camp at Ayers Rock. Gibson did not come back, and Giles never saw him again.

In 1876, Giles set off again from Adelaide, but this time he took camels with him instead of horses. He reached Perth on the west coast. Then, he returned to Adelaide and became the first man to make the crossing in both directions.

The North American Desert

The southwest of the United States is not regarded by most people today as a desert like the Sahara Desert or the Gobi Desert. There are many areas that are very hot and very dry, but there are also grasslands, or **prairies**, to the north. The first explorers called all of this area the Great American Desert. This was because they could not find enough water to farm the land or to live there safely.

The Two Expeditions

The Spanish settlers from Mexico were the first to explore the southwest of America. In 1539, travelers told stories about the Seven Cities of Cibola. These cities were said to be full of gold. The Spaniards planned two expeditions. One group was to go up the west coast by sea in several small ships. This group was led by Pedro Alarcón. He did not find any gold, but he did map the Gulf of California.

The other group went by land with 300 men and 1,000 horses. This group was led by Francisco Coronado.

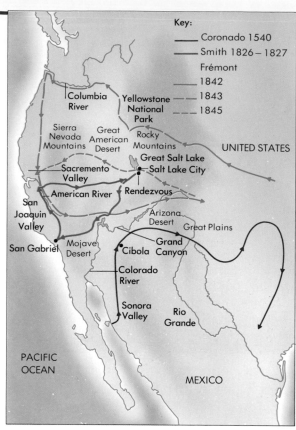

▲ The routes of Francisco Coronado, Jedediah Smith, and John Charles Frémont.

▶ Francisco Coronado came from Mexico. In 1540, he led an expedition into the American southwest in search of the Seven Cities of Cibola. American Indians had said that these cities were rich in gold, but Coronado never found any.

Coronado's Journey

In 1540, Coronado's men rode northward. They went up the Sonora Valley into southern Arizona. His group traveled over 1,500 miles of mountains and deserts. Coronado wrote that they saw "grey lions and leopards." These may have been cougars and wildcats. When they found Cibola at last, there were no golden cities. There were only the villages of the Zuni people. These people did not welcome strangers and their attacks slowed down the men as they moved north.

▼ The largest herds of elk now live in Yellowstone National Park. In Coronado's time, they roamed across the United States.

Coronado's group reached the Grand Canyon. They spent the winter in a village in the Santa Fé Mountains. There, they were told of gold farther north. In the early spring, the group moved on. They traveled across the Great Plains, which were full of elk and deer. From there, they moved on into Texas and found herds of buffalo. The group could find no gold.

In a last attempt, Coronado led a group into Oklahoma. The Spaniards saw the good black soil, but they wanted gold and not farm land. Then, Coronado returned to Mexico. His group had not found any gold to the north.

Jedediah Smith

Three hundred years passed before new settlers began to explore the southwest of the United States. The first American to travel in the western deserts was Jedediah Smith. Smith was a **trapper**, and he had spent three years in the forests near the Rocky Mountains.

In the early 1800's, California was part of Mexico. The only way to the west coast was along the Columbia River to the north.

▲ A trapper with his horse and furs in the Rocky Mountains.

▲ Jedediah Smith was looking for fur trade routes across the Rocky Mountains. He was the first to cross from the Great Salt Lake along the Colorado River to San Diego. He also made the first land exploration of Oregon and Washington. He was killed in 1831 on the Santa Fé trail.

A Journey to the Southwest

In August, 1826, Smith and a group of trappers left a town called Rendezvous near Great Salt Lake. They were looking for beaver. The group crossed southern Nevada. On their route, they could not find any beaver nor any water. The men struggled on, and to their surprise they came across a green valley. This was the land of the Mojave people. These people fed and took care of Smith and his men. They sold horses to Smith and guided his group across the dry Mojave Desert. At last, on November 27, Smith and his men arrived at the Mission of San Gabriel at the western edge of the desert.

The Return to Rendezvous

The Mexican governor of California heard about Smith's journey. He was worried that Americans would find a route overland to California. They could then use it to attack the Mexicans.

Smith wrote to him to explain the reason for his journey. The governor told him to go back across the Mojave Desert. Smith agreed but when he got fifty miles inland, he turned north.

After traveling about 300 miles the group came to the American River area. At last, they found hundreds of beaver. It was now May, 1827. Smith split his group. He would go ahead with two men and seven horses. The others would wait for his return.

Smith and his men set off over the Sierra Nevada Mountains. It was very cold as they climbed over the mountains. Four of the horses died, and the men were weak from cold and hunger.

At last, the men reached the grasslands and found water. They had traveled over 1,875 miles and found a way through to California.

Smith went back to California to find his men. They all returned safely to Rendezvous. In the next hundred years, milions of people moved into California. Few people used Smith's route through the mountains because the route was not good for wagons. However, Smith's maps and writings about his travels helped others to settle in the southwest.

▲ The Grand Canyon in the Arizona Desert with the Colorado River at the bottom. The first desert explorers who saw the Canyon were Francisco Coronado and his men in 1540.

Explorers and Settlers

About 150 years ago, pioneers began to move west to look for new land to farm and to settle in. The explorers had opened up new routes across the mountains and the deserts. The farmers and traders followed them when they heard there were passable trails and good land to be found. The United States government sent people to find this new land. Many of the explorers who were sent were in the army and knew about making maps. One of these men was John Charles Frémont.

Frémont the Pathfinder

In 1842, Frémont went on his first journey to the Rockies. He mapped the area around Great Salt Lake. A year later, Kit Carson, the well-known mountain man joined him and others to explore the Columbia River. Then, the group crossed the Sierra Nevada Mountains in winter. The snow made this a very hard journey. One man went crazy and a number of men suffered from **snow blindness**. They could not see where to put their feet safely to make the next step. When the men got through to California, they mapped the Sacramento Valley. The group then went south through the San Joaquin Valley and returned eastward through Colorado.

▲ A pioneer wagon train. The covered wagon was a home for the pioneers, and it carried all their belongings. The journey across the Great American Desert was over 1,875 miles and it could take up to three months. It was a rough and dangerous journey. The early pioneers thought the desert land was poor. Later, people realized that it was good farm land.

▲ John Charles Frémont explored and mapped much of the area between the Rocky Mountains and the Pacific Ocean. He helped produce the first scientific maps of the American West. He once ran for President of the United States, but he lost.

On his third trip in 1845, Frémont and his group went through Nevada across the Sierra Nevada Mountains. From there, they went into California. Frémont's maps and the story of his journey were very useful in helping people to settle on the west coast. The United States government printed thousands of copies of the story of his journey. People read these and planned their new life in the West. Frémont was called the "Pathfinder."

Frémont as Governor

In 1846, the United States Army fought the Mexicans and won. California became part of the United States. Frémont knew the routes across the Sierra Nevada into California. He helped with the **conquest** of this new state. Then, he became the first governor of California. It was men like Frémont who proved that much of the area called the Great American Desert was good land. People could settle and farm there.

The End of an Age

What desert areas are left for pathfinders to explore? Today, we have strong trucks and planes to cross the deserts. Most of these areas are well mapped. The true explorers of the future will look to the moon and planets for new deserts to map and explore.

◄ Deserts are no longer such difficult places to cross. Today, we have cars, planes, and maps. The early explorers had to rely on horses, camels, the desert people, and their own courage.

Quiz

How much can you remember about this book? Try this quiz. Use your index and glossary to help you to find the answers.

1. Here are some names of famous desert explorers with the letters scrambled. Unscramble the letters to find the explorers' correct names.

    a) MITHS, b) SLIGE, c) SWILL,
    d) DORNOCOA, e) STRUT, f) KURBE,
    g) GRISETHE, h) HOTESPAN

2. Can you guess what this sentence says in full?

    "There are _____ birds _____,
    and no _____ below.
    There is _____ water nor _____
    to be found."
    Clue: A Chinese monk said this about the Gobi Desert.

3. Put the following events in the order in which they took place:
    a) Burke and Wills make the south to north crossing of Australia.
    b) Bertram Thomas crosses the Empty Quarter.
    c) Francis Younghusband enters the city of Lhasa.
    d) Lady Hester Stanhope visits Palmyra.
    e) Hsuan-Tsang starts out alone across the Gobi Desert.

4. Match the descriptions (a) to (f) with the words (1) to (6) below them.

    a) People who move around a lot in the desert
    b) A group of traders traveling with camels in the desert
    c) A holy city of Islam
    d) The largest desert in Africa
    e) Hills of sand in the desert
    f) Fertile areas in the desert

    1) the Sahara
    2) oases
    3) caravan
    4) nomads
    5) dunes
    6) Mecca

5. Complete the following sentences with (a), (b), (c), or (d).

    1) Hsuan-Tsang crossed the
       a) Sahara Desert.
       b) Arabian Desert.
       c) Gobi Desert.
       d) Sturt Desert.

    2) Which of these desert travelers crossed the Empty Quarter?
       a) Robert Burke
       b) Harry Philby
       c) Francis Younghusband
       d) Alexandrine Tinné

    3) Kano is a city in
       a) Australia.
       b) America.
       c) Asia.
       d) Africa.

    4) Cooper's Creek is in
       a) Africa.
       b) Arabia.
       c) Australia.
       d) the United States.

5) Jedediah Smith was a
   a) soldier.
   b) trapper.
   c) diplomat.
   d) sailor.

6. How many desert explorers can you find with names beginning with B, S, or T?

7. Which desert would you be in if

   a) it stretched from the Red Sea to the Persian Gulf?
   b) it was the largest in the world?
   c) the Druze lived there?
   d) you were in Asia and surrounded by mountains to the north, south, and west?
   e) you were close to the mission of San Gabriel?

8. Who or what

   a) is "the great traveler of Islam?"
   b) is used to make gunpowder?
   c) went with a dyed face to Kano?
   d) carried two iron tanks filled with water across the Sahara?
   e) entered Mecca with an Egyptian named Mehemet Ali?

9. Are these statements True or False?

   a) The Blunts bought horses in the Gobi Desert.
   b) Burckhardt traveled in West Africa.
   c) A holy journey is called a pilgrimage.
   d) Frémont became the first governer of California.
   e) John Stuart crossed Australia from south to north.

Glossary

Aborigine: the name for one of the people living originally in Australia. It comes from a Latin word meaning "from the beginning."

algae: very simple plants. Algae have no leaves, roots, or stems. Most algae are found in water.

barren: describes land in which nothing will grow.

base: a place from which an organization or expedition works and keeps its main supplies.

blizzard: a snowstorm blown by a very strong, cold wind.

Buddhism: the religion of the Buddhists who follow the teachings of Buddha.

caravan: a group of people and their camels traveling across the desert.

Ceylon: an island in the Indian Ocean, off the southeast coast of India. The name of the island was changed to Sri Lanka in 1972.

chieftain: the leader or ruler of a group of people or a tribe.

continent: a large mass of land, usually including many countries. The earth is divided into seven continents.

conquest: the act of overcoming or defeating an enemy.

crater: a bowl-shaped hollow in the ground made by an explosion, or a large object from space.

creek: a stream.

desert: an area of dry land which has little or no rainfall. Plants cannot grow in deserts easily.

diplomat: a person who represents his or her own country in another country.

disguise: to change one's appearance by wearing different clothes or makeup.

expedition: an organized journey which is made for a special purpose. Explorers went on expeditions to find out about other lands.

foreigner: a person who belongs to another country.

gulf: a part of the ocean or sea which goes into the land in a wide deep bay or channel.

Islam: the religion of the Muslims which follows the teaching of Muhammad.

keg: a small barrel.

merchant: a person who buys and sells goods, often dealing with other countries.

meteorite: a piece of rock or metal from space which has crashed into the earth.

monk: a man who lives in a religious group.

millet: a type of grass which produces seeds that can be eaten.

musket: a type of long-barrelled gun fired from the shoulder. Muskets were used in the 1700's and 1800's by soldiers and hunters.

Muslim: someone who follows the religion of Islam and the teachings of Muhammad.

nomad: someone who moves about from place to place in search of food or to find grass for animals. Nomads do not make their homes in one particular place.

oasis: a place in the desert where underground water comes to the surface and plants can grow.

Palastine: the name for the historic area between the Jordan River and the Mediterranean Sea. It is now the country of Israel.

peak: the top of a mountain.

pilgrim: a person who makes a journey to a holy or special place.

pilgrimage: a journey to a holy or special place.

porter: a person who is hired to carry goods.

prairie: a large, open area of grassland without trees. The grasslands of North America are called prairies.

preserve: to stop something from rotting or spoiling. Today food is often preserved by canning or freezing.

ration: an amount of food divided into portions among people.

region: a district or an area.

remote: describes something which is far away from other places. A remote island is a long way from other land.

route: the way to get from one place to another. Routes are shown on maps and plans.

saltpeter: a white powder used for making gunpowder or fireworks. Saltpeter is also used as a fertilizer.

sand dune: a hill of sand built by the wind.

sandstorm: a desert wind storm which carries along clouds of sand.

scurvy: a disease caused by the lack of vitamin C. This disease leads to bleeding of the gums and damage to the teeth and bones.

sheik: the head man or leader of a group of Arabic people.

snow blindness: a condition of the eyes which makes them red and very sensitive to light. Snow blindness is caused by the eyes receiving too much reflected light from ice and snow.

stud farm: a place where horses are kept for breeding purposes.

sultan: the ruler of a Muslim country.

supplies: the food, fuel, or equipment required for an expedition.

swampy: describes wet, soft ground.

telegraph line: bundle of insulated wires which are used to carry telegraph messages.

temperature: the measure of how hot or cold something is. Thermometers are used to measure temperatures.

trader: someone who does business by buying and selling goods.

trapper: a person who sets traps to catch animals for their fur.

treasure: a collection of precious metals and stones, like gold and diamonds.

vitamin C: a substance which is found in foods such as fresh vegetables and fruit. Vitamin C is essential for good health.

wading bird: long-legged birds that live near water.

walkabout: one of the periodic journeys made by Aborigines into the bush in Australia.

wasteland: an area not suitable for living on or for any other purpose.

water bag: a bag made out of animal skin. Water bags were used for carying water across deserts.

Index